MW01241660

CHRISTIANS

MEET

ISRAEL

30 DAY DEVOTIONAL BY:

THIS DEVOTIONAL BELONGS TO:

Maryline

A GIFT

FROM:

Dot

OCCASION:

2022 Grape Harvest

DATE:

24 August 2022

9-3-22 Tulsa Int Airport
Dot & I are off on

ACKNOWLEDGMENTS

Blessed be God Almighty for His great mercy towards Israel and His loving kindness towards all those who call upon His name! Thank You Lord for being faithful, for restoring Israel, for revealing truth from Your Word and for enabling me to write about Your goodness.

Thank you Dad and Mom (Tommy & Sherri Waller) for your courage in pioneering this path in understanding and for taking an active role in what God is doing in Israel.

A huge thank you to all those who have served and are serving as staff at HaYovel. Pioneering isn't easy. Because of your sacrifices, Israel is being restored and the nations are connecting to the land and people of Israel!

Special thanks to all those from the nations who have put their love for Israel into action by serving on the mountains of Israel with HaYovel. You are changing the world!

This devotional is dedicated in memory of

William Hechler

for his great devotion as a Christian Zionist
to the Jewish people.

CONTENTS

INTRODUCTION

DAY ONE - God Loves Israel

DAY TWO - God's Covenants Stand Forever

DAY THREE - Does God Show Favoritism

DAY FOUR - The Blessing of Abraham

DAY FIVE - Bless Israel

DAY SIX - Your Kingdom - on EARTH

DAY SEVEN - Grafted into Israel

DAY EIGHT - Yeshua was a Zionist

DAY NINE - Yeshua was a Jew

DAY TEN - Yeshua was a Settler

DAY ELEVEN - Every Tribe and Tongue

DAY TWELVE - Yeshua Son of David

DAY THIRTEEN - Yeshua Came to Israel

DAY FOURTEEN - Yeshua's Disciples did Jewish Stuff

DAY FIFTEEN - Jewish-Christian Relationship

CONTENTS

DAY SIXTEEN - Oracles of God

DAY SEVENTEEN - A Nation Born in a Day

DAY EIGHTEEN - The People Return

DAY NINETEEN - Hebrew Restored

DAY TWENTY - Vineyards Restored

DAY TWENTY ONE - Cattle Restored

DAY TWENTY TWO - The Nations Will Come

DAY TWENTY THREE - Israel Unearthed

DAY TWENTY FOUR - Rebuilding the Ancient Ruins

DAY TWENTY FIVE - Nations Will Pray

DAY TWENTY SIX - Nations Will Remind

DAY TWENTY SEVEN - Pray For Jerusalem

DAY TWENTY EIGHT - Come to Israel

DAY TWENTY NINE - Support Israel

DAY THIRTY - Be an Ambassador for Israel

CONCLUSION

RESOURCES

Foreword

We have heard it over and over as people experience the land of Israel: "I will never look at the Bible the same way again!" I am thankful for the awakening God brought to our family as we stepped into the calling to tangibly support the prophetic return of the Jewish people to their promised inheritance. As the Executive Director of HaYovel, Zac is carrying a huge weight on his shoulders. The age-old burden of replacement theology is not bringing the horrific violence it did over the last 2000 years. Today the burden comes in the form of indifference which may not seem as destructive but in many ways is much more devastating. Will Christianity ever be able to shed this debilitating weight and recognize the undeniable move of God occurring in this generation?

Sherri and I have been blessed with eleven children who possess unique gifts and abilities that God is using and will use to advance His Kingdom. In this thirty day devotional, Zac has used his gifting to put together a scriptural foundation that will challenge us to throw off our indifference and become zealous for what God is zealous for.

Tommy Waller
President and Founder
HaYovel

Introduction

For 2,000 years, Israel had become completely desolate. For Christians, any seed of hope that Israel might reclaim her God-given role, was crushed by all prominent pastors and theologians. Israel was simply irrelevant - long lost in the annals of history as the place that was once God's capital on earth.

Yet, Israel's resurrection in 1948 produced a major shift. The Israel question could no longer be left in the recesses of bygone days. The words of God spoken by prophets three thousand years ago were being fulfilled in perfect detail! This reality has pushed theologians back to the drawing board, pastors to the Bible and all Christians to fear the God of Heaven who is faithful to His promises.

Now the question is, how does this phenomenon affect you as a Christian? Do you have some responsibility in this miraculous move of God? Is there a need for you to be informed and connected?

So many questions arise.

Why did God choose a land and people?

God created the entire world. Does He show favoritism to Israel?

How does Yeshua (Jesus) fit into this narrative?

Was Yeshua a Zionist?

God has resurrected the literal nation of Israel. How should we, as Christians, relate to it? Is this just a fulfillment of God's promises to care for the Jewish people or is it possible that the Kingdom of God is literally coming to Earth? If so, what does that mean?

How should we relate to God's Chosen people? Are they still Chosen? If so, what does that mean for them and, more importantly, what should their Chosenness mean to us?

This thirty day devotional is your key to answering those questions and many more! Please take time every day to read, study and pray as you make your way through the following pages.

Blessings on your journey,

Zac Waller
Executive Director
HaYovel

DAY ONE

"Again the word of the Lord of hosts came, saying, 'Thus says the Lord of hosts: "I am zealous for Zion with great zeal; with great fervor I am zealous for her."'"
Zechariah 8:1-2 NKJV

GOD LOVES ISRAEL

The number one duty of a Christian is to submit ourselves to God. Our Father in Heaven has called us to put off our dreams, lifestyles and desires and begin a journey of embracing His. Old things have passed away, behold all things have become new! Being reconciled to God means that we are also realigned with Him.

God loves Israel. There's no doubt about that. The Scriptures are replete with verses declaring that God is greatly, fervently zealous for the literal land of Israel.

The title "Israel" can refer to a specific location, a specific people or the entire people of God. In today's verse, God uses "Zion". Biblically, "Zion" is one very specific location.

Theologies created by those who didn't live to see Israel's literal restoration have greatly inhibited many Christians from embracing what God loves. We must choose to agree with God's choosing. The miracles that are happening in Israel are the loving hand of our Faithful God!

ACTION QUESTION

What changes do I need to make in order to fully love what God loves
and be in full alignment with His will?

NOTES

1. I have to be in his word to see how he
communicates with, Will to Lean & Do Believe
his promises he has made to me & who ever
accept him. Talk to him ask Don't take for granted
Repent imedially

DAY TWO

"Thus says the Lord: If I have not established my covenant with day and night and the fixed order of heaven and earth, then I will reject the offspring of Jacob and David my servant and will not choose one of his offspring to rule over the offspring of Abraham, Isaac, and Jacob. For I will restore their fortunes and will have mercy on them."
Jeremiah 33:25-26 ESV

GOD'S COVENANTS STAND FOREVER

Even though Israel has miraculously been resurrected, "replacement theology" (or "supersessionism") is still alive and well in the Church.

The basic tenets of this theology are that the physical land of Israel has been replaced by a spiritual, heavenly land and the Jewish people have been replaced by the Church as God's chosen. In some ways it is understandable. Seeing Israel desolate for thousands of years would make one question whether the prophecies of Scripture are literal or only spiritual.

However, the literal restoration of Israel, taking place exactly as prophesied, declares to the world that God's will and His word are both spiritual and literal, down to the last detail!

Bottom line: God does not go back on His covenants!

ACTION QUESTION

Do I maintain perspectives that have been influenced by replacement theology? Does my relationship with the Jewish people and the Land of Israel reveal agreement with or rejection of Replacement theology?

NOTES

The are his promised people   He loves them
Some are turning to Yoshua   It is up to them

DAY THREE

"For thus says the Lord of hosts: 'He sent Me after glory, to the nations which plunder you; for he who touches you touches the apple of His eye.'"
Zechariah 2:8 NKJV

DOES GOD SHOW FAVORITISM?

If God created the entire world, then why is Israel the apple of His eye? What if I have a heart for Africa? Does that mean I'm not aligned with God?

Israel was chosen for a specific purpose - to be a light to the nations! God wants everyone in the world to be reconciled to Him. He chose Israel to be the theater, the launching pad for redemption to reach the entire earth.

Jerusalem becoming a "praise in all the earth" (Isaiah 60:7) means that the knowledge of God covers the earth.

If you have a heart for Africa, you should take the message of Israel to Africa. Africans need to be introduced to the God of Israel - the God that is faithful to His promises!

Israel is the centerpiece, the matrix, the epicenter from which God reaches out to all the nations of the earth!

Sept 8

ACTION QUESTION

In what ways can I incorporate the message of Israel into my outreach to the needy and broken of this world? Why is this important?

NOTES

_____

_____

_____

_____

_____

_____

_____

_____

_____

_____

_____

_____

_____

_____

_____

_____

DAY FOUR

"Now the Lord had said to Abram: 'Get out of your country, from your family and from your father's house, to a land that I will show you. I will make you a great nation; I will bless you and make your name great; and you shall be a blessing. I will bless those who bless you, and I will curse him who curses you; and in you all the families of the earth shall be blessed.'"
Genesis 12:1-3 NKJV

THE BLESSING OF ABRAHAM

Though Adam was the first man, and Noah saved humankind from the flood, the title "father" was given to Abraham. Through his faith and obedience, our father Abraham began a movement that will eventually reconcile all the families of the earth back to God.

The book of Galatians chapter three verse eight says that God preached the Gospel to Abraham. The mission of global redemption was first given to Abraham and that is the Gospel!

What was the first step in this plan of salvation? Go to Israel! A physical land and a literal people were chosen by God for the sake of the world. The land of Israel is a critical component in God's master plan of salvation for the world.

ACTION QUESTION

God does a lot of choosing throughout Scripture. Am I willing to submit to His decisions on who and where He has chosen, even if I don't completely understand why?

NOTES

_____

_____

_____

_____

_____

_____

_____

_____

_____

_____

_____

_____

_____

_____

_____

_____

_____

Day Five

"I will bless those who bless you, and I will curse him who curses you; and in you all the families of the earth shall be blessed."
Genesis 12:3 NKJV

Bless Israel

English translations use the word curse twice in this verse. The Hebrew actually uses two different words. The first "curse" in the verse is from the Hebrew word "arar" which means "to put a curse on." The second "curse" is from the Hebrew word "kalal" which means "to lightly esteem."

So, taking the differences of those two words into consideration, the verse could be read: "I will bless those who bless you, and I will put a curse on him who lightly esteems you; and in you all the families of the earth shall be blessed."

The verse is therefore not saying that if we speak curse words about Israel then God will put a curse upon us. It is saying that if we ignore or if we are indifferent towards Israel, then we will be cursed.

It is time for believers to honor Israel and walk in the blessing of God, given through our father Abraham!

ACTION QUESTION

In what ways do I lightly esteem the Jewish people or the Land of Israel? What can I do to bless, honor and serve them?

NOTES

_____

_____

_____

_____

_____

_____

_____

_____

_____

_____

_____

_____

_____

_____

_____

_____

_____

Day Six

"When you pray, say:
'Our Father in heaven, hallowed be Your name. Your kingdom
come. Your will be done on earth as it is in heaven.'"
Luke 11:2 NKJV

Your Kingdom Come - On Earth

Because of their belief in replacement theology, theologians were forced to spiritualize any Scripture references to the Kingdom of God on earth. All the passages in Scripture that mentioned the restoration of a literal, physical land were twisted to mean some mystic location out in the cosmos.

This theological position has led to belief in a God that is impossible to relate to, a desire to escape earth as soon as possible and a complete detachment of the spiritual from the physical. This detachment has caused many to plunge headlong into immorality.

An honest look at the teachings of Yeshua reveals that He preached a Kingdom that brought earth and heaven together, on earth!

There is simply no other way to describe the miracles that are taking place in Israel today. God is bringing His Kingdom to earth, exactly as Yeshua instructed us to pray!

ACTION QUESTION

Am I actively bringing God's Kingdom to earth? In what ways have I missed seeing God's purpose for the physical and literal realities of life on this earth?

NOTES

_____

_____

_____

_____

_____

_____

_____

_____

_____

_____

_____

_____

_____

_____

_____

_____

DAY SEVEN

"And if you are Messiah's, then you are Abraham's seed, and heirs according to the promise."
Galatians 3:29 NKJV

GRAFTED INTO ISRAEL

Not only did God choose a literal land but He also chose a people group - Israel, a nation with real flesh and bones.

The people of Israel were tasked with restoring God's presence to planet Earth. The ultimate goal is to get back to the garden of Eden, where all of mankind can walk with God.

The path to redemption has certainly been an unexpected route. As Paul puts it: "Oh, the depth of the riches both of the wisdom and knowledge of God! How unsearchable are His judgments and His ways past finding out!" (Romans 11:33)

It is important to learn and know about the people of Israel because, if you have chosen Yeshua as your Savior, you are now part of the family of Israel! You have taken on the family vision and are now responsible for bringing the rest of the world into the family.

ACTION QUESTION

If I am part of the family of Israel, what opportunities have I taken to treat the Jewish people like brothers and sisters?

NOTES

_____

_____

_____

_____

_____

_____

_____

_____

_____

_____

_____

_____

_____

_____

_____

_____

_____

_____

_____

Day Eight

"Therefore, when they had come together, they asked Him, saying, 'Lord, will You at this time restore the kingdom to Israel?' And He said to them, 'It is not for you to know times or seasons which the Father has put in His own authority.'"
Acts 1:6-7 NKJV

Yeshua was a Zionist

Yeshua's disciples had been at His feet, listening to Him preach about the coming Kingdom. After forty days of learning, the disciples had one question: Are you going to do the things that you have been teaching us, right now? Are you going to restore the Kingdom of God in Israel, today?

Yeshua's answer was that it was not yet time. That means that one day, it will be time!

"Zionism", is generally defined as an international movement dedicated to the cause of re-establishing a Jewish national and religious community in Israel.

Yeshua is the ultimate Zionist! He knows that one day God will release Him to reign from the literal, physical city of Jerusalem on Mount Zion.

In that day, Jerusalem will be a praise in all the earth and the promise made to Abraham will be completely fulfilled - all the families of the earth will be blessed!

ACTION QUESTION

As a Christian, I have given my life to serve Yeshua. Have I taken the time to get to know Him? Who is He? What does He stand for? What are His dreams for us and the planet?

NOTES

_____

_____

_____

_____

_____

_____

_____

_____

_____

_____

_____

_____

_____

_____

_____

_____

_____

DAY NINE

"The book of the genealogy of Yeshua Messiah (Jesus Christ),
the Son of David, the Son of Abraham:"
Matthew 1:1 NKJV

YESHUA WAS A JEW

Before launching into the complete genealogy of Yeshua, in the very first verse of the New Testament, Matthew declares that Yeshua is the son of David and the son of Abraham. Why is that important? Shouldn't the fact that Messiah has arrived override the need to reference any other leaders?

Abraham began the movement. God said that Abraham would become a great nation and that all nations would be blessed through him.

David was a King of Israel - the fruition of the promise that Abraham's seed would become a great nation. He was also a foreshadow of Messiah - a king reigning over a unified Israel dedicated to God's service.

Yeshua is the Messiah, the coming King of Israel and the fruition of the promise to Abraham that all the families of the earth would be blessed through him. Through Yeshua we are brought into the movement that Abraham started!

ACTION QUESTION

If Abraham and David are intricately connected to who Yeshua is, do I
know enough about them to know who Yeshua is and what He came
to do?

NOTES

_____

_____

_____

_____

_____

_____

_____

_____

_____

_____

_____

_____

_____

_____

_____

_____

_____

_____

Day Ten

"Joseph also went up from Galilee, out of the city of Nazareth, into Judea, to the city of David, which is called Bethlehem... with Mary, his betrothed wife, who was with child... So it was... she brought forth her firstborn Son, and wrapped Him in swaddling cloths, and laid Him in a manger."
Luke 2:4-7 NKJV

Yeshua was a Settler

Messiah, the light of the world was born in Bethlehem, Israel! We must not overlook the fact that Yeshua is an Israeli, Jewish settler who was born to observant Jewish parents, in a Jewish, Israeli settlement located in what Israel-haters have renamed the "West Bank."

Biblically, the so-called "West Bank" is the eastern side of Jerusalem, Judea and Samaria. This is the biblical heartland of Israel where eighty percent of the Bible was either written or occurred!

Every place in Scripture where God says, "To your descendants I will give this land," happens in this very area, with one exception - God spoke to Isaac in Gerar, which is modern day Gaza. Isn't that a coincidence!

Furthermore, every piece of land whose purchase is documented in the Bible is located in this very same area.

ACTION QUESTION

When I hear people say "West Bank" what comes to my mind? How can I educate myself more on these biblical areas?

NOTES

_____

_____

_____

_____

_____

_____

_____

_____

_____

_____

_____

_____

_____

_____

_____

_____

_____

_____

_____

DAY ELEVEN

"So they came to Jerusalem. Then Jesus went into the temple and began to drive out those who bought and sold in the temple, and overturned the tables of the money changers and the seats of those who sold doves. And He would not allow anyone to carry wares through the temple. Then He taught, saying to them, 'Is it not written, "My house shall be called a house of prayer for all nations"? But you have made it a den of thieves.'"
Mark 11:15-17 NKJV

EVERY TRIBE AND TONGUE

Yeshua knew that His Father's house was a very special place. Even as a boy, he knew where he wanted to be - in His Father's house, doing His Father's business!!

Instead of selling their wares down off the Temple Mount, the merchants had brought their goods up onto the precincts of the Mount itself. This area was known as the "Court of the Nations" and was specifically designated for non-Jewish people to come and worship the God of Israel. No wonder Yeshua quoted this verse from Isaiah! These shop owners were inhibiting the nations from coming up to worship His Father!

We, together with our Messiah, Yeshua, are still awaiting the day when every tribe, tongue and nation will come and worship God in the literal, physical location of Mount Zion in Jerusalem, at the Holy Temple!!

ACTION QUESTION

If the Temple was restored today would I go worship God there, fulfilling Yeshua's dream for His Father's House?

NOTES

where is it? church

Day Twelve

"I, Yeshua, have sent My angel to testify to you these things in the churches. I am the Root and the Offspring of David, the Bright and Morning Star."
Revelation 22:16 NKJV

Yeshua Son of David

Complete spiritualization of biblical texts have extracted the literal, physical realities from prophecy, but it hasn't stopped there. This hyper-spiritual, "God is only in the cosmos and earth is a necessary evil that we must escape" mentality has also affected our view of Yeshua. Yes, Yeshua is divine, but He is also fully human.

Yeshua could have said, "Let the Churches know that I am the eternal, all-seeing, all-knowing, heavenly force that will reside in your innermost being throughout the ages, no matter where you are in the world." But He chose to say, "I am the Offspring of David." He is the "Lion of the tribe of Judah" and He is returning with that identity!

If we hate Jews, Jewish things, Jewish culture, Jewish law or Jewish tradition, then we may well find ourselves hating the one we claim to be Messiah when He comes! If we have chosen a Jewish Lord and Master and have decided to follow Him, then we should not only follow Him in His divinity but also in His humanity. He is our example in both!

ACTION QUESTION

Am I offended at the Jewishness of Yeshua? Are there any remnants of anti-semitism that I need to purge from my life, perspectives or actions?

NOTES

_____

_____

_____

_____

_____

_____

_____

_____

_____

_____

_____

_____

_____

_____

_____

_____

_____

Day Thirteen

"Now after Jesus was born in Bethlehem of Judea in the days of Herod the king, behold, wise men from the East came to Jerusalem, saying, 'Where is He who has been born King of the Jews? For we have seen His star in the East and have come to worship Him.'"
Matthew 2:1-2 NKJV

Yeshua Came To Israel

Abraham heard the Gospel (Galatians 3:8) and went to Israel. Jacob did not remain in Haran but returned to Israel. The nation of Israel could not fulfill their destiny to bring salvation to the world if they stayed in the land of Egypt, which they had just conquered. All of God's prophets were from Israel. Yeshua the Messiah was born in Israel and, with the exception of a quick childhood trip to Egypt, never left!

It is quite obvious that the literal, physical, geographical location of the land of Israel has been chosen by God to be a catalyst of light and salvation to the world.

After two thousand years, the process of restoration has begun! A few of the bulbs on the "Israel-lighthouse-beam" have been repaired. More are being restored every day. Those who desire to see and help others see the way of redemption, acknowledge the light of the Land! Go see it, share its source and let the world know how to find it!

ACTION QUESTION

What am I doing to rekindle and project Israel's redemptive beam to the world?

NOTES

_____

_____

_____

_____

_____

_____

_____

_____

_____

_____

_____

_____

_____

_____

_____

_____

_____

_____

Day Fourteen

"And they devoted themselves to the apostles' teaching and the fellowship, to the breaking of bread and the prayers."
Acts 4:42 ESV

Yeshua's disciples did Jewish stuff

A lot of mainstream Christianity promotes a mindset that Yeshua and His disciples started a new religion and rejected all Jewish culture, tradition and religion. In order to support that notion, we would never see Yeshua or his disciples keeping any Jewish tradition. Correct?

In Acts we see that the disciples continued in THE prayers. "The prayers" refer to the liturgical prayers prayed daily by all devout Jews. Yeshua's custom was to go to synagogue (Luke 4:16). He apparently had a good relationship with the Pharisee leaders in Capernaum (Luke 7). Timothy is circumcised (Acts 16). Paul proves that he keeps the law (Acts 21). Paul states the "unbiblical" Jewish tradition that Jannes and Jambres resisted Moses, as fact!

Yeshua and His disciples were not only Jewish but they also acted like Jews! Should we then take on everything Jewish? No. We should, however, respect and learn from the Jewish tradition, law and customs that the Jewish people keep.

ACTION QUESTION

Am I quick to jump to the conclusion that Jews are wrong? Have I taken the time to talk to them and learn why they do what they do? If I'm honest, am I seeking truth or am I bashing Jews and operating in some level of anti-semitism?

NOTES

_____

_____

_____

_____

_____

_____

_____

_____

_____

_____

_____

_____

_____

_____

_____

_____

Day Fifteen

*"Let all those who hate Zion
be put to shame and turned back."*
Psalm 129:5 NKJV

Jewish/Christian Relationship

Unspeakably gruesome crimes have been committed against the Jewish people in the name of Yeshua. From the Crusades to the pogroms to the Inquisition and the Holocaust, millions of Jewish men, women and children were brutally tortured and murdered. All of these used Christian theologies as their basis of hatred for the Jews.

"Those people weren't true Christians," or, "We can't take responsibility for all those horrific things!" are common Christian responses.

These things were done in the name of Yeshua. It is imperative for us to bring reparation to His name! Because He has been so grossly misrepresented and His name attached to such heinous evils, we must take action to rectify this horrible wrong. Actions were done to cause the harm and actions must be done to heal the wounds.

In the end, all those who hate Zion will receive their just punishment. Let us not be counted among them!

ACTION QUESTION

What am I doing to bring honor back to the horrifically marred name
of Yeshua?

NOTES

_____

_____

_____

_____

_____

_____

_____

_____

_____

_____

_____

_____

_____

_____

_____

_____

_____

DAY SIXTEEN

"What advantage then has the Jew, or what is the profit of circumcision? Much in every way! Chiefly because to them were committed the oracles of God. For what if some did not believe? Will their unbelief make the faithfulness of God without effect? Certainly not!"
Romans 3:1-4 NKJV

ORACLES OF GOD

Christians owe an enormous debt to the Jewish people. They have meticulously preserved the holy Scriptures for thousands of years. Where would we be without God's word?

The Jewish people have also given us the Messiah!

The very existence of the Jewish people is a declaration to the world that God is faithful. As Mark Twain put it "...Peoples have sprung up, and held their torch high for a time, but it burned out and they sit in twilight now or have vanished. The Jew saw them all, beat them all, and is now what he always was, exhibiting no decadence, no infirmities of age, no weakening of his parts, no slowing of his energies, no dulling of his alert and aggressive mind. All things are mortal, but the Jew. All other forces pass, but he remains. What is the secret of his immortality?" (Mark Twain: *Concerning the Jews, Point No. 6., March, 1898,* Harpers Magazine.)

God made the Jews "immortal" in order to fulfill His word and to bring the gift of salvation to the entire world!

ACTION QUESTION

Have I ever held gratitude in my heart towards the Jews? In what ways can I show them my deep appreciation?

NOTES

_____

_____

_____

_____

_____

_____

_____

_____

_____

_____

_____

_____

_____

_____

_____

_____

_____

_____

Day Seventeen

"Who has heard such a thing? Who has seen such things? Shall the earth be made to give birth in one day? Or shall a nation be born at once? For as soon as Zion was in labor, she gave birth to her children."
Isaiah 66:8 NKJV

A Nation Born in a Day

In the days of old it was impossible to simply declare statehood. Kings would fight battles that would take at least a few months, maybe many years. At the end of the battle, the conqueror was obvious and sovereignty was declared.

The prophets saw a day coming that would be different. Somehow, a nation would come into existence in a single day!

On May 14th, 1948, the words of Isaiah came to pass and David Ben Gurion declared that the nation of Israel was a sovereign Jewish state. He finished his speech with, "Placing our trust in the Rock of Israel, we affix our signatures to this proclamation at this session of the provisional council of state, on the soil of the homeland, in the city of Tel-Aviv, on this Sabbath eve, the 5th day of Iyar, 5708 (14th May, 1948)." (David Ben Gurion: *Declaration of Establishment of State of Israel,* May, 1948, Israel Ministry of Foreign Affairs, Foreign Policy.)

The nation of Israel was born in a single day!

ACTION QUESTION

Am I willing to acknowledge that the rebirth of Israel is indeed from God and not from man? If it is from God and I am God's child, in what ways should I be affected by and connected to His doings?

NOTES

_____

_____

_____

_____

_____

_____

_____

_____

_____

_____

_____

_____

_____

_____

_____

_____

_____

Day Eighteen

*"'I will bring back the captives of My people Israel;
they shall build the waste cities and inhabit them;
they shall plant vineyards and drink wine from them;
they shall also make gardens and eat fruit from them. I will
plant them in their land, and no longer shall they be pulled up
from the land I have given them,' says the Lord your God."*
Amos 9:14-15 NKJV
Also see: Isaiah 11:11-12 & Deuteronomy 30:1-6

The People Return

It is really no wonder that the literality of these types of Scriptures
were brought into question. For thousands of years the land of Israel
lay desolate. The people of Israel were scattered throughout the
entire earth. Every other nation who had experienced much less
tragic fates were quickly assimilated, their lands enveloped by
neighboring countries, their names and culture limited to the confines
of historical documentation.

True to the more than fifty prophecies in Scripture, in the late 1,800's,
the literal people of Israel began to be reunited with their physical
ancient homeland, exactly the way the prophets of God foretold
thousands of years before! In the year 1800 there were approximately
7,000 Jews living in Israel. In 1914 the census shows 94,000. 2019
statistics show 6,774,000! The total 2019 population, including Jews,
Muslims, Christians, etc… was 9,092,000.

ACTION QUESTION

How does this "greater exodus" (Jeremiah 16:14-15) affect me? What can I do to fulfill Isaiah 49:22?

NOTES

_____

_____

_____

_____

_____

_____

_____

_____

_____

_____

_____

_____

_____

_____

_____

_____

_____

Day Nineteen

"For then I will restore to the peoples a pure language,
that they all may call on the name of the Lord,
to serve Him with one accord."
Zephaniah 3:9 NKJV

Hebrew Restored

Once again, many speculated that this prophetic "pure language" must be referring to something very spiritual. Perhaps it could be the chant of a monk, speaking in tongues, or maybe it could be a supernatural cleansing from filthy language.

Then, on January 7th, 1858, Eliezer Ben Yehuda was born. Like the dawning of a new day, the light of the restored Hebrew language began to shine. On October 13th, 1881, Eliezer and his friends made a pact to speak only Hebrew. By the early 1900s Hebrew had been restored to the streets of Israel.

If the modern day events aren't enough to prove that Hebrew is Zephaniah's "pure language," there's also a very interesting literary phenomenon in the Hebrew text. Every single letter of the Hebrew alphabet, including all the letter variations, are found in verse 8. This heralding verse builds up and launches right into: "Then I will restore a pure language"!

ACTION QUESTION

In what ways am I participating in this part of the redemption and learning the language of Heaven?

NOTES

_____

_____

_____

_____

_____

_____

_____

_____

_____

_____

_____

_____

_____

_____

_____

_____

_____

_____

Day Twenty

"But you, O mountains of Israel, you shall shoot forth your branches and yield your fruit to My people Israel, for they are about to come. For indeed I am for you, and I will turn to you, and you shall be tilled and sown."
Ezekiel 36:8-9 NKJV

Vineyards Restored

The years of Israel's exile were endured with the hope that God's presence would return to Israel. The first sign - branches shooting forth from the mountains! The prophet Jeremiah goes into specifics about what type of branches could be expected: "You shall yet plant vines on the mountains of Samaria; the planters shall plant and eat them as ordinary food." (Jeremiah 31:5)

The people of Israel knew that grape vines planted on the mountains of Samaria were a sure sign of God's favor and the coming redemption. It is therefore no coincidence that, a thousand years later, our Redeemer's first act of redemption was turning water into wine!

For two thousand years, there were no vineyards on the mountains of Samaria. Today, the mountains are replete with beautiful vineyards, flowing from the mountain peaks down into the valleys. Thousands of tons of prophetic grapes are harvested every single year!

ACTION QUESTION

Am I taking notice of the seemingly mundane miracles that are happening around me? What about the ones in Israel?

NOTES

_____

_____

_____

_____

_____

_____

_____

_____

_____

_____

_____

_____

_____

_____

_____

_____

_____

Day Twenty One

"Thus says the Lord: 'In an acceptable time I have heard You, and in the day of salvation I have helped You; I will preserve You and give You as a covenant to the people, to restore the earth, to cause them to inherit the desolate heritages; that You may say to the prisoners, "Go forth," to those who are in darkness, "Show yourselves." They shall feed along the roads, and their pastures shall be on all desolate heights.'"
Isaiah 49:8-9 NKJV

Cattle Restored

Western culture has become increasingly removed from familiarity with agriculture and farming. It is therefore difficult for us to associate salvation, restoration, captives set free and light overcoming darkness with cattle feeding along the road and green pastures on what were desolate heights - unless you come to Israel and see the reality of it with your own eyes!

It is amazing to see the spiritual realities of God's restoration of His land and people being carried out in such simple, humble ways. To see rocky, barren mountain heights that have obviously been desolate for thousands of years slowly turning back to green, lush pastures is reason to praise God for His faithfulness!

ACTION QUESTION

In what ways does God confirm His salvation to me? When am I taking time to listen?

NOTES

_____

_____

_____

_____

_____

_____

_____

_____

_____

_____

_____

_____

_____

_____

_____

_____

_____

Day Twenty Two

"Strangers shall stand and feed your flocks, and the sons of the foreigner shall be your plowmen and your vinedressers."
Isaiah 61:5 NKJV

The Nations Will Come

Had God only accomplished the impossibility of taking what was desolate and returning it to life, we would have seen enough to acknowledge His great faithfulness, but He did not stop there! He also transformed the hearts of the nations, who for centuries had tortured the Jewish people, to desire to love, bless and serve Israel!

It is happening today! Thousands of people from all over the world are coming to Israel to take part in the miraculous redemption of Israel. Exactly as the prophets foretold, these God-serving, Israel-loving people are showing up with hearts to humbly serve Israel in whatever way they can. Many are actually serving as vinedressers!

Thousands of tons of grapes have been harvested by these volunteers. They provide quality work, hearts of love and a positive international voice while connecting to the land of their faith, restoring Jewish-Christian relations and gaining an understanding of God's purposes for Israel.

ACTION QUESTION

Am I willing to sacrifice whatever it takes to go to Israel and fulfill this role of the nations, or will I miss this hour of God's visitation?

NOTES

_____

_____

_____

_____

_____

_____

_____

_____

_____

_____

_____

_____

_____

_____

_____

_____

_____

_____

DAY TWENTY THREE

"Awake, awake! Put on your strength, O Zion; put on your beautiful garments, O Jerusalem, the holy city! For the uncircumcised and the unclean shall no longer come to you. Shake yourself from the dust, arise; sit down, O Jerusalem! Loose yourself from the bonds of your neck, O captive daughter of Zion!"
Isaiah 52:1-2 NKJV

ISRAEL UNEARTHED

Archeologists have uncovered a plethora of ancient ruins throughout the length and breadth of Israel. Many biblical cities - cities that God-haters have sworn never existed - have been discovered. Atheists have quite a dilemma on their hands when the facts on the ground overwhelmingly prove their worst nightmare. Many have come to faith simply by witnessing the evidence firsthand.

Israel is truly "shaking off her dust"! What was hidden is being revealed. It is truly amazing to see how God carefully tucked away ancient Israel, meticulously preserving the ancient ruins just below the surface of the ground. Earth-shattering discoveries have been made just a few feet down from where people have been walking for centuries.

The incredible thing is that this is happening now! God has chosen to reveal His secrets in our day! What a privileged generation we are!

ACTION QUESTION

How am I staying abreast of the happenings in Israel?

NOTES

_____

_____

_____

_____

_____

_____

_____

_____

_____

_____

_____

_____

_____

_____

_____

_____

_____

_____

DAY TWENTY FOUR

"And they shall rebuild the old ruins, they shall raise up the former desolations, and they shall repair the ruined cities, the desolations of many generations."
Isaiah 61:4 NKJV

REBUILDING THE ANCIENT RUINS

The unprecedented mass volume of Jewish immigration to their ancestral homeland naturally led to the fulfillment of the prophetic rebuilding of the ancient ruins.

Some joke that the "crane" is Israel's national bird. It is true that there are always cranes busily hoisting building materials in cities all throughout Israel. The land is being built up again!

In Har Bracha, a Jewish community in Samaria, there is a waiting list of people who would like to move into the community. Despite the community's incessant building of new apartments, they cannot keep up with the demand!

It is inspiring to see aerial shots of Israel. Just a few years ago there were barren hillsides and small towns. Now there are huge thriving cities with immaculate landscaping. Search online for a photo of Tel Aviv in 1920. You will be inspired by what has happened in just 100 years, after 2,000 years of desolation!

ACTION QUESTION

Millions of people stand against the Jewish people building houses and repopulating the biblical heartland of Israel. Are they alone or will I do something about it?

NOTES

_____

_____

_____

_____

_____

_____

_____

_____

_____

_____

_____

_____

_____

_____

_____

_____

Day Twenty Five

"Also the sons of the foreigner who join themselves to the Lord,
to serve Him, and to love the name of the Lord, to be His
servants— everyone who keeps from defiling the Sabbath,
and holds fast My covenant— even them I will bring to My
holy mountain, and make them joyful in My house of prayer."
Isaiah 56:6-7 NKJV

Nations Will Pray

The nations have a very positive role to play in their relationship with Israel. Not only are they to come and serve in the miraculous restoration of the land, but they are also to worship God in the place that He has chosen!

This "worship-on-location" element is so important that God Himself takes on responsibility for the travel arrangements. He says, "I will bring them!"

There are a myriad of testimonies declaring God's supernatural provision to those whose hearts burn with zeal to love, serve, and pray with Israel. Thousands of people are showing up from the four corners of the earth and fulfilling the words of the prophets. This astounds those who attempt to deny that the restoration of Israel, and the international involvement in it, is God's doing.

ACTION QUESTION

How is my zeal-ometer looking? Is it high enough to get me to Israel? What time slots have I set aside for prayer and study in order to keep my zeal levels up?

NOTES

_____

_____

_____

_____

_____

_____

_____

_____

_____

_____

_____

_____

_____

_____

_____

_____

_____

DAY TWENTY SIX

*"When the Lord brought back the captivity of Zion,
we were like those who dream. Then our mouth was filled with
laughter, and our tongue with singing. Then they said among
the nations, 'The Lord has done great things for them.' The
Lord has done great things for us, and we are glad."*
Psalm 126:1-3 NKJV

NATIONS WILL REMIND

As the nations come flooding in to bless, support, and pray in Israel, another biblical phenomenon is occurring.

The Jewish people have seen a lot. They have survived some of the worst atrocities known to man. Though mocked, ridiculed, tortured and killed, they remained true to their faith in God and the belief that one day He would bring redemption to Israel.

They held onto the hope that one day they would, as the psalmist says, be returned to their land to dream, laugh and sing. But what happens before they say, "The Lord has done great things for us"? The nations say, "The Lord has done great things for them!"

When the nations, who have historically crucified the Jews, acknowledge that it is God who is with Israel, then Israel will realize that it is God who has saved them!

ACTION QUESTION

What opportunities do I have to tell the Jewish people that God has
done great things for them?

NOTES

_____

_____

_____

_____

_____

_____

_____

_____

_____

_____

_____

_____

_____

_____

_____

_____

_____

DAY TWENTY SEVEN

"Pray for the peace of Jerusalem:
'May they prosper who love you...'"
Psalm 122:6 NKJV

PRAY FOR JERUSALEM

Israel is special and chosen by God for a very unique purpose. How do I connect to and join God in what He is doing through her? The very first step is to pray!

Pray that God would conform your heart to His. If He is greatly fervently zealous for Zion (Zechariah 8), pray that He would help you have those same emotions.

Pray that God would bless Israel to be the light they are called to be in this world, that God would use Israel to make His name known in all the earth!

Pray that Israel's enemies would be put to shame and turned back (Psalm 128) and that the lies that are being told would not be believed.

Pray that all the restorative things that God has promised to Israel would come to pass.

There are many Scriptures that declare God's promises to Israel. It is powerful, as Daniel the Prophet exemplifies, to remind God of His promises!

ACTION QUESTION

How is my Israel prayer schedule looking? What is my prayer goal?

NOTES

_____

_____

_____

_____

_____

_____

_____

_____

_____

_____

_____

_____

_____

_____

DAY TWENTY EIGHT

"Thus says the Lord of hosts:
'In those days ten men from every language of the nations
shall grasp the sleeve of a Jewish man, saying, "Let us go with
you, for we have heard that God is with you."'"
Zechariah 8:23 NKJV

COME TO ISRAEL

The reality that God is doing something in Israel couldn't be more obvious! If God is with them, then our response should be to "go with" them.

"Going with" could mean not resisting, humbling ourselves, listening to them, or just acknowledging that what is happening in Israel with the Jewish people, is God and not just some fluke accident of natural occurrences that are happening in the land of Israel.

The straight forward, simple meaning is to literally go to the Holy Land. In today's time it is amazingly possible to get to Israel. What are your priorities? Do you want to go? Make the choice to consider Jerusalem your highest joy (Psalm 137:6) and God will make a way!

There are so many opportunities to serve in the land. Do your research and don't just go on a tour. Go get your hands dirty! Join God as He brings restoration to His land and people. You will never be the same!

ACTION QUESTION

What are God's plans for my "going with" journey?

NOTES

_____

_____

_____

_____

_____

_____

_____

_____

_____

_____

_____

_____

_____

_____

_____

_____

_____

_____

Day Twenty Nine

"Then everyone came whose heart was stirred, and everyone whose spirit was willing, and they brought the Lord's offering for the work of the tabernacle of meeting, for all its service, and for the holy garments."
Exodus 35:21 NKJV

Support Israel

If your heart is stirred and your spirit is willing, bring an offering! Give financially towards God's work in Israel. Just as the Tabernacle of old was to bring the presence of God into the camp of the Israelites, so now Israel is bringing God's glory into the whole world.

This could mean selling some of your assets to give, setting apart a tithe every month or offering a skill that God has given you.

If you cannot physically go, a great way to give is to provide the finances for someone else to go. It could be someone in your congregation or a long distance friend.

Please be sure to get to know a ministry before you give. Are they serving Israel, or are they peddling their own agenda? Are they operating with integrity? Are they successfully accomplishing what they say they are accomplishing? Do they have a good reputation in Israel?

ACTION QUESTION

Does my pocketbook show a willing heart to love Israel? Should I set aside money monthly for this cause?

NOTES

_____

_____

_____

_____

_____

_____

_____

_____

_____

_____

_____

_____

_____

_____

_____

_____

_____

DAY THIRTY

"But Joshua the son of Nun and Caleb the son of Jephunneh... spoke to all the congregation of the children of Israel, saying: 'The land we passed through to spy out is an exceedingly good land. If the Lord delights in us, then He will bring us into this land and give it to us, a land which flows with milk and honey.'"
Numbers 13:6-9 NKJV

BE AN AMBASSADOR FOR ISRAEL

The message of the ten spies is blaring on high volume at every frequency imaginable. They are saying, "The giants (terrorism, replacement theology, liberal mindset, etc...) are too tall (convincing), and there's no way that God can be faithful to His word (atheism, agnosticism)."

The Joshuas and Calebs of this generation are rising to the occasion and speaking out as bold ambassadors for God and Israel. With no fear of being singled out and ridiculed, no thought to pain or even death, not an ounce of wavering faith, these courageous men and women are standing firmly on God's promises and they will not be moved!

Will you rage with the nations? Will you join the crowd that has lost its faith in God or will you take your stand with the Joshuas and Calebs, for such a time as this!

ACTION QUESTION

What opportunities do I have, right where God has me now, to be a positive voice for Israel and the Jewish people?

NOTES

_____

_____

_____

_____

_____

_____

_____

_____

_____

_____

_____

_____

_____

_____

_____

_____

_____

Conclusion

Thank you for making your way through the "Christians Meet Israel" Devotional. My hope is that you were encouraged and challenged by what you have read.

May God give you supernatural wisdom to know how to answer the questions you have come upon in this book. May He grant you the gumption to take action in a world that glorifies indifference.

May we see the coming of the King of Glory to His throne on Mount Zion and may every tribe, tongue and nation come and worship Him in the beauty of holiness!

God's richest blessings be with you and your family as you continue your journey with Him,

Zac Waller
Executive Director
HaYovel

Resources

Want to volunteer in Israel?
- www.serveisrael.com

Want to keep up with what is happening in Israel?
- Articles: www.IsraelHeartlandReport.com
- Podcast: The Joshua and Caleb Report (on all main podcast platforms)

HaYovel's Mission

Millions of people are actively fighting against the miraculous regathering of the Jewish people and the restoration of their land.

HaYovel brings Christian volunteers from around the world to serve Israel's farmers. We provide quality work, hearts of love, and a positive international voice.

Our volunteers connect to the land of their faith, restore Christian Jewish relations, and gain an understanding of God's purposes for Israel.

The UnseenRealm Documentary
-Dr Michael S Heiser   Logos Bible Softw

Is

Made in the USA
Columbia, SC
14 September 2020